PILGRIM · GUIDE

✠

CANTERBURY

Also available in the *Pilgrim Guide* series

PILGRIM · GUIDE

CANTERBURY

Peter Brett

Residentiary Canon of Canterbury Cathedral

Illustrated by
John Doyle

President of the Royal Watercolour Society

CANTERBURY
PRESS
Norwich

Text © Peter Brett 1997
Illustrations © John Doyle 1997

First published 1997 by The Canterbury Press Norwich
(a publishing imprint of Hymns Ancient & Modern Limited
a registered charity)
St Mary's Works, St Mary's Plain.
Norwich, Norfolk, NR3 3BH

British Library Cataloguing in Publication Data

A catalogue record for this book is available
from the British Library

ISBN 1-85311-164-3

Typeset, printed and bound in Great Britain by
The Lavenham Press Ltd,
Lavenham, Suffolk, CO10 9RN

For Gill

Then Jacob awoke from his sleep and said, 'Surely the Lord is in this place, and I did not know it!' And he was afraid and said, 'How awesome is this place! This is none other than the house of God, and this is the gate of heaven.'

[Jacob's Dream:
Genesis 28: 16–17, *NRSV*]

When using this guide in the Cathedral, it may be helpful to follow the visitors' path set out on the Welcome leaflet, available at the west end of the Nave.

The guide is intended to be used reflectively and read at the positions in the Cathedral indicated on the plan on p. x.

Contents

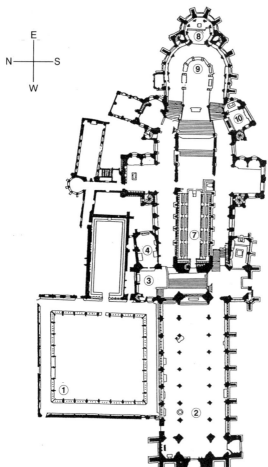

1. The Great Cloister
2. The Nave
3. The Martyrdom
4. The Chapel of
   Our Lady Martyrdom
7. The Quire
8. The Corona
9. The Trinity Chapel
10. St Anselm's Chapel

Introduction

The story of Christ Church Cathedral, Canterbury, reaches across the centuries from the moment of St Augustine's arrival on the coast of Kent in the year AD 597 to the present day. Even before St Augustine, the first Archbishop, Christians worshipped here in a church during the Roman occupation of Britain. It was the remains of this church which were given by the local King Ethelbert to Augustine, the missionary monk sent by Pope Gregory. Here, as the Archbishop he was soon to become, his symbolic seat was set, and here his successors have kept their seats ever since. The present Archbishop, George Carey, is the 103rd incumbent. The Cathedral is now the Mother Church of the Anglican Communion of Churches throughout the world joined with the See of Canterbury.

The Cathedral's story is one of unbroken and continuous witness to Christianity and the upholding of faith in God's life in his world. Here, at different times, different kinds of community have lived and offered worship – not only through the dedication of their individual members, but also under the obligation of a corporate discipline.

In the Saxon centuries after Augustine, regulated groups of clergy attended on the Archbishops. At the end of the 10th century we find that a closer society had become established, living a monastic life under the Rule of St Benedict. This was dissolved, along with all the other monastic houses of the land, in the 16th century, and in 1541 a new foundation, under a Dean and Chapter (of Canons) was formed by Royal Charter.

The formal core of worship, common to this long history, has been the recitation of the Offices of each day and the offering of the Eucharist. This formality has been permeated and enriched by the varying personal spirituality of individual members, in meditation, in contemplation and in intercession, as well as in teaching and nurturing others in the Christian way of life – a way of life which has never left unnoticed and unheeded the needs of a suffering world and the pain and anxiety of human existence.

Here is a place of many holy archbishop-saints – Augustine, Theodore, Dunstan, Alphege, Anselm, Thomas and Edmund. Their holiness was characterized not by the false piety which separates from the world, but by the application of their Christian convictions to human affairs – none more so than Thomas, whose martyrdom in this, his own Cathedral, in 1170, at the same time shocked Christendom and won its acclaim.

It was this martyrdom which began the tradition of visiting and pilgrimage, which today amounts to some two million people each year. The constant flow brings many who are touched, perhaps for the first time in their lives, by a sense of otherness given to them by this place. It may be the effect of amazing architecture, or an experience of worship, or a feeling of awe and personal insignificance, or the power of history. Whatever and howsoever it may be, the sensation is of a holy place of divine presence. People make new resolves, in consequence; some realize gratitudes and blessings, long unacknowledged; others are given new perspectives and hopes. Few are unaware of the value of serenity and peace, and many are given vision and guidance.

Sometimes it seems as though the very buildings themselves are at prayer. Perhaps that should not be too surprising in a place where for so long God and his people have met.

*   *   *

A figure from the canopy of the tomb of King Henry IV

O go your way into his gates with thanksgiving,
     and into his courts with praise: be thankful
unto him and speak good of his name.

For the Lord is gracious, his mercy is everlasting:
and his truth endureth from generation to generation.
                              [Psalm 100: 3,4 *BCP*]

1

The Great Cloister

Living around a square enclosure is an idea not only to be
found in monastic establishments. In the medieval world,
be it the community of a charitable hospice, or the society of
an academic institution, a quadrangle comprising church or
chapel, hall or refectory, and residential accommodation
was commonplace as a secure and practical way of
expressing the identity and continuing workings of a body
corporate.

In Canterbury's Great Cloister, we are surrounded by the
elements which constituted the life of a Benedictine house.
Dominating everything on the south side is the nave of the
great church with its three graceful towers. The church is
rightly dominant, because the regular round of worship
known as the 'Opus Dei' (literally, 'the work of God') is the
first of the responsibilities of a monastic household.

On the east side is the Chapter House, so called because
each day, at the gathering of the community, the focus of
attention was the reading of a chapter of the Rule of
St Benedict under which they lived. To the north, on the east
side, above the Cloister, can be seen the remains of the
Romanesque Great Dormitory. Along the side opposite to
the church was the Refectory. In front of its 14th-century
entrance, two bays of the internal cloister arcading were
adapted to accommodate the water cisterns and basins at
which the monks washed before going in to meals. They are
beautifully embellished and much of the original painted
decoration remains.

In the corner nearby, a door with a little hatch to the left
of it led into the stores of the Cellarer, the monastic house-
keeper. The hatch was a place where a monk, with good

The bays of the Great Cloister, adapted for ablutions

reason, might get extra refreshment.

The existing Cloister was finished in 1414. It was laid out originally by Archbishop Lanfranc in the 11th century and then partly restyled in the 13th century before its final updating as we see it now. You can see in the walls the scant respect paid by successive builders to the work of their predecessors. Nevertheless, we are left with lovely vistas as we walk along the 'panes', as they are called. Overhead, the 15th-century vault is decorated with heraldic devices – the most extensive collection of the time to be found in England. The last arms to be inserted, in the south-west corner, include those of Pope John Paul II and Archbishop Robert Runcie, commemorating the Pope's visit in 1982. A third new one is that of the Prince of Wales, who presided over the Cathedral Appeal Committee at the time.

The Cloister was a place of concentrated activity – all conducted under the restraint of the 'Lesser Silence' of the monastic day. In the pane alongside the church the novices were instructed and reading was taught and practised. A certain amount of manuscript work went on there, though a more comfortable Scriptorium was elsewhere.

Comings and goings from the Chapter House would have included great occasions, such as the election of an Archbishop or a Prior, as well as the day-to-day ordering of the life of the community. Inside we look up at the magnificent ceiling, made of oak imported from Ireland and constructed in 1405. It is a very large room, made much longer than Lanfranc's original plan by extension in the 13th century, when it was surrounded by the present arcading.

The Prior presided at Chapter. While the Archbishop was technically the Abbot, it was in title only, and the Prior ruled with his senior officials, known as 'Obedientiaries' – Sub-Priors, Cellarer, Precentor, Sacrist, Treasurers, and Penitentiary. Their responsibilities covered both domestic matters and also the external affairs of the properties and estates of the monastery. The Prior himself was a significant political figure, involved in the secular affairs of the nation. We have to remember that the sacred and the secular were not separated in the medieval mind and practice as they have come to be today.

Then, as now, a group of people endeavouring to live a corporate life of dedication and service, did not do so without normal human problems and weaknesses. There were disputes and differences; members behaved and misbehaved; penalties and punishments were imposed, as permitted by the Rule. In rare and extreme cases, a brother might be expelled from the monastery altogether.

It was, however, the genius of balance and evenness which lay at the heart of the Rule of Benedict. Three factors formed the framework of the monastic day – prayer, study and work. Each was to be, so far as possible, in equal proportion, and developed in harmony with the others. 'So, let everything be done at the proper time' [Rule 47.1]. It is the appeal of this sense of balance, order and dedication that has led many contemporary writers to interpret the Rule of St Benedict for use by ordinary Christians as a basis for an even, sane and godly life in today's world.

The very large Chapter House corresponds with the generous proportions of the Cloister and the Quire of the church itself. Lanfranc had the vision of a big establishment of 150 monks, though usually there were about eighty.

There are three kinds of cathedral in England. There are the non-monastic 'Old Foundations', so called because they retain the characteristics of their pre-Reformation life. Constituted originally of a dean and prebends, they were refounded in the 16th century and continued much as before. The second category is that called the 'New Foundations'. These were newly formed at the Reformation, changing from monastic to non-monastic, yet keeping many of the characteristics and governance of their former existence. Dean and canons replaced Prior and monks. As well as this there were some other New Foundations made for newly formed 16th century dioceses. Most of these were housed in old monastic churches. The third group are called the 'Modern Foundations'. These have come into being from the 19th century onwards, and were created to house the seats of the bishops of recently formed dioceses, using existing parish churches.

Canterbury is a New Foundation. Its life and worship are governed by its Statutes, originally granted by Royal Charter in 1541 and revised from time to time to meet new circumstances.

*　　*　　*

We believe that the divine presence is everywhere and that 'the eyes of the Lord are looking on the good and the evil in every place'. But we should believe this especially without any doubt when we are assisting at the Work of God. To that end let us be mindful always of the Prophet's words, 'Serve the Lord in fear' and 'In the sight of the angels I will sing praise to you.'

[Rule of St Benedict, Chapter 19. 1-5]

2

The Nave

The sheer grace and majesty of this space is breathtaking. The geometry is a masterpiece of simplicity and yet the symmetry is incomparable. It was the King's master-builder, Henry Yvele, who designed this structure to replace the old Romanesque nave of Archbishop Lanfranc, demolished in 1377. It took twenty-eight years to complete, and a change in the colour of the stone, two feet or so above the mid-height rings on the soaring shafts of the central columns, shows where works were halted for several years because of lack of funds and manpower. Finally, in 1405, the vault was completed – a ribbed vault, with linking 'liernes', splaying the rising arcades into a canopy of such delicacy as to give the impression of some avenue of close-set trees. It is one of the finest expressions in Europe of 'high-Gothic' architecture – a concept which strove to achieve a sense of heaven upon earth.

The medieval rood-screen in the western arch of the crossing tower has long since gone and one is struck by the fact that, without it, in the actual architecture, almost no Christian symbolism is left. And yet, what could more powerfully speak of the perfection of God than the proportions and sublime unity of this space?

The existing Nave is set on the foundations of Lanfranc's cathedral (1070–77). Below the paving-stones are the remains of the earlier structures on this site – the evidence of four generations of Saxon cathedrals, uncovered when the floor was renewed in 1994. They were seen to represent a surprisingly massive building, befitting the importance of this site for English Christianity.

The South aisle of the Nave

10

The Pulpitum Screen (1455), set at the top of the flight of steps to the east, is framed and given perspective under the strainer arch which spans the last columns of the Nave arcade – the same columns which are the massive western piers of the central (Bell Harry) tower. This great arch is one of several, set between columns in support of the central tower. Viewed from below, from different positions, they form an intricate and beautiful relationship of angles and curves and stresses. And yet they were not intended in the original design. In the building of the last section of the central tower, finished in 1498, weaknesses became evident in the south-west pier and the supporting network of arches was put in place. Grace and beauty were born of emergency and necessity.

The royal figures in the screen give away the Lancastrian sympathies of the monastery during of the Wars of the Roses – a dangerous allegiance at the time! From the left they are: Richard II, Henry V, Ethelbert (the 6th-century founder), Edward the Confessor (benefactor of the English Church and patron saint of the Lancastrian house), Henry IV and Henry VI.

As if to emphasize the essentially secular character of the Nave, the monuments along the walls are mostly of lay people, many military, and all post-Reformation. Notable among them on the north side are the memorial to Hadrian de Saravia (1595–1612), one of the translators of the Authorized Version of the Bible, and that of the great English composer, Orlando Gibbons (1585–1625).

On the south side is the monument of William Grant Broughton, first Bishop and Metropolitan of Australia (1834–53) and nearby, to the right, is commemorated James Beaney (1828–91), a member of the Legislative Council of Australia and benefactor of this city. Sir George Gipps (1791–1847), Governor of New South Wales, is on the left.

As first conceived, this great hall of the Nave was to be the ante-room of the court, as it were. Beyond the screen was the court itself, in permanent attendance on God, in worship and praise. Over the court God's own throne was set – the altar with the consecrated bread and wine, the sacrament of his presence, suspended in its special container, a pyx, high above. In the Nave, as pilgrims and visitors, God's people assemble and make ready to move on through the sacred spaces.

An altar always stood to the east to accommodate the immediate spiritual needs of the people as they arrived. The font (1639) and pulpit (1898) came later as the Nave became a space used more generally for great services, though both had medieval predecessors. It is a busy place, nearly always thronged with visitors. At great national observances it is filled with the great and the ordinary, in common mourning or joy, offered to God in penitence or thanksgiving. On the Christian festivals Jesus is glorified in his birth, death and resurrection by large numbers of worshippers filling this space. It is here that the world and its God meet.

The west window contains some of the oldest stained glass. The central panel of the bottom row shows Adam, at work in the Garden of Eden. It is the earliest of our pieces and dates from 1178. It is flanked by depictions of other figures taken from the long line of Old Testament characters who comprised the human ancestry of Jesus' family. Others in this genealogical set are in the middle row. They were removed in the late 18th century from their original positions in the clerestory of the Quire, with yet others which are now to be found in the south window of the south-west transept, and were replaced later with copies. The rest of the glass in this particular window belongs to the time when the Nave was built.

A nice link is to be made between the lovely, ancient

figure of Adam in the glass panel, and the font. Both convey truths of creation. Human beings owe their origination to God's love – a love which is disclosed and renewed at the time of re-creation when we come to new life with Christ through the sacrament of Holy Baptism.

*　　*　　*

Hear the supplications of your servant and of your people Israel when they pray towards this place. Hear from heaven, your dwelling-place; and when you hear, forgive.

[King Solomon's Prayer at the Dedication of the Temple at Jerusalem, c. 950BC: 2 Chronicles 6: 21, *Revised English Bible*]

3

The Martyrdom

On 29th December, 1170, as the community was singing Vespers, the Archbishop, Thomas Becket, was pursued into his Cathedral and murdered in the north-west transept. Christendom was appalled and the King, who willed his destruction, was to be humiliated. Thomas's last words were, 'I accept death for the name of Jesus and his Church.' Within days, cloths soaked in his blood were being claimed to have miraculous powers. The Church was given a new martyr who, in little over two years, was to be declared a Saint.

*The Cross of
the Martyrdom*

A sculpture now marks the fatal spot. With the addition of its shadow, it represents the four swords of the violent knights who cut down the Archbishop: Reginald Fitzurse, Richard de Brito, Hugh de Morville and William de Tracy.

They thought to ingratiate themselves with their King and ended by glorifying his enemy – the one whom they destroyed.

In our own time, the poet T. S. Eliot, inspired by this martyrdom at Canterbury, has written:

> A Christian martyrdom … is always the design of God, for His love of men, to warn them and to lead them, to bring them back to His ways. It is never the design of man; for the true martyr is he … who no longer desires anything for himself, not even the glory of being a martyr.
>
> [*Murder in the Cathedral*, Faber 1935]

The text of St Thomas's last sermon in the Cathedral had been the portentous words:

> For here we have no lasting city, but we are seekers after the city which is to come.
>
> [Hebrews 13:14, *Revised English Bible*]

The listening monks felt a premonition of his death, observing that it seemed 'as if his heart burned within his very countenance.'

Few of the stones which now surround this sacred spot actually witnessed the death of Thomas. Much of the Romanesque structure was scoured out in the 13th century, and more was to follow in the 15th century. The original 11th-century staircase, rising in the corner, looked down on the scene. The base stones of the original pier which are behind the modern altar, and a few fragments in the floor butting up to them, still remain; and that is about all. The old 'Altar of the Sword's Point', together with all other memorabilia of Thomas – throughout the land, as well as in the Cathedral – were swept away by royal command in 1538. Relics, pilgrimage and shrines were out of favour. Another King, Henry VIII, had taken the opportunity to settle the 368-year-old score of his predecessor.

But even before Henry VIII set about his destructive work on the Church – much of which was to assert his political power – the falling off of the popularity of pilgrimages had begun to influence respect for the fabric of erstwhile venerated spaces. However it was, the architectural alterations to this area were sweeping, until finally the lofty transept vault high above the holy place was formed in the later 15th century.

The Martyrdom is a place where one is made aware of the often conflicting claims of God over against those of the world. The original devastating event itself was a momentous crisis in a struggle for political control. It was to do with the boundaries of divine and secular authority in the courts and affairs of state. Then at the Reformation – whatever the theological issues – the King took the opportunity to reclaim lost political ground. To destroy the cult of Thomas at Canterbury was a chance to destroy a powerful, national focus of ecclesiastical superiority.

Clearly God's rule is yet to be established and his Kingdom is yet to come, and the Church is but an imperfect instrument in working to achieve it. But this place of the Martyrdom is a sacred spot which defies obliteration. It draws us into an atmosphere of continuing tension as we stand, unable to avoid its discontent.

The tomb of Archbishop William Wareham nearby emphasizes the point. It was he who, in 1532, presided over the Convocations of the English Clergy which received the Act of the Submission of the Clergy, whereby they acknowledged the authority of the King in all ecclesiastical causes. They submitted, but in a profound silence!

Next to him lies the body of Archbishop John Peckham. His Franciscan vows to a simple life of poverty and devotion contrast strongly with worldly claims of power. In his time, in the 13th century, the community here was in danger of losing its discipline and order. His example did much to bring the Priory back to the course of its rightful allegiance.

It was entirely fitting that another momentous event in the history of the Church was arranged to take place here, in the Martyrdom, on 29th May 1982. Pope John Paul II and the then Archbishop of Canterbury, Robert Runcie, knelt together in silent prayer. A new element was brought into the atmosphere of this holy space – that of reconciliation. The events of the 16th-century Reformation inevitably left raw wounds in the body of the universal Church – many caused by the struggles for power, to which human beings seem so prone, and whose consequences remain in this place. For the first time in history a reigning Pontiff had come to England and in this place prayed for the uniting of Christian people within the embrace of the love of God. Nothing could be more effective in pointing us back to where the priorities of our values should lie.

*   *   *

Then Jesus told his disciples, 'If any want to become my followers, let them deny themselves and take up their cross and follow me. For those who want to save their life will lose it, and those who lose their life for my sake will find it. For what will it profit them if they gain the whole world but forfeit their life? Or what will they give in return for their life?'
[Matthew 16: 24-6, *NRSV*]

17

4

The Chapel of Our Lady Martyrdom

What a glorious and exuberant extravaganza of architecture this Chapel is! The crockets and finials and tabernacle-work and fan-vaulting have been brought to such a pitch of perfected fragility as almost to threaten their own survival. Ribs and niches and cusps and quatrefoils abound. Apart from the deprivations of the Puritans in the 17th century – of which, thankfully, little evidence remains – the delicate carved stonework is left remarkably intact after five centuries. Only the sculptured saints are lost.

Perhaps times of great human need, such as those in which we live, make us neglect the need of the spirit for release into generosity and the sheer joy of giving for its own sake. A pity, because such release is an important characteristic of the worship of God. Not for nothing are the rising mouldings of the arcading and the superb frieze behind the altar set with angels whose wings are poised to rustle with joyful movement.

The original Romanesque structure of this space was of two levels. The upper was dedicated to St Blaise and the lower to St Benedict. In the great rebuilding works of the 15th century, it was decided to remove the Lady Chapel, which occupied the easternmost bays of the north aisle of the Nave, into these renovated and grander quarters. The new Chapel had its own boys' choir and choir-master, who daily sang the Office of Our Lady from wooden stalls on each side. There is a nice thread of continuity in the modern day-to-day offering in the Quire of Choral Evensong – the successor to monastic Vespers – which is now a treasured and popular aspect of Cathedral worship. In that service the Magnificat – the Song of the Blessed Virgin Mary – is a carefully preserved and constant element. The Chapel is used today for the said daily office of Morning Prayer offered corporately by the Cathedral clergy.

Christians have long sought the companionship of Jesus' mother in their devotions. Her sorrows and her joys, as we reflect on them in traditional Marian devotions, reflect so powerfully the stress of human relationships. Basil the Great (in the 4th century) speaks of her as the 'joy of all creation', because of all created things, it was she who was chosen for the uniquely sacred task of carrying the incarnate God. By means of the process of human birth, God showed himself to be at one with his world.

*   *   *

You never enjoy the world aright, til the sea itself floweth in your veins, til you are clothed with the heavens, and crowned with the stars; and perceive yourself to be the sole heir of the whole world; and more than so, because men are in it who are every one sole heirs as well as you. Til you can sing and rejoice and delight in God, as misers do in gold, and kings in sceptres, you never enjoy the world.

Thomas Traherne
c 1636–74

*   *   *

The 15th-century screen of the Chapel of Our Lady Martyrdom

The bronze figure of St Benedict recalls the original dedication of the lower Chapel here. In his hand he holds his Rule for Monasteries, inscribed with its opening word 'Obsculta' ('Listen'), the first requirement of one who would pray. Under the plain common sense of the balanced devotion of this Rule, the community here lived from the 10th to the 16th century. Many of the basic principles of the Rule persist in the spirit of the Cathedral community today, as well as in its liturgy and worship.

Both the figure of St Benedict (1986) and that of the Blessed Virgin Mary (1982) were sculpted by Mother Concordia OSB of Minster Abbey in Thanet.

Tombs in this Chapel are those of early deans of the 16th and 17th century. The demise of the popular cult of the Blessed Virgin Mary in post-Reformation times led to the Chapel being called 'The Dean's Chapel' for several centuries.

The angel from the Chapel of Our Lady Martyrdom

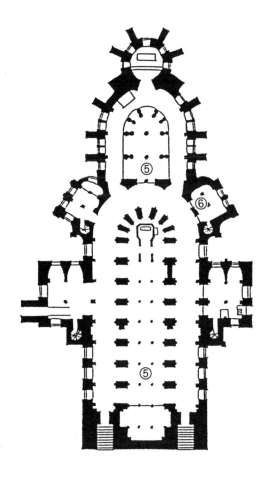

The Crypt

5 The Crypt
   (Western and Eastern)
6 St Gabriel's Chapel

5

The Crypt

The Crypt is a very still place. It lies in the depths of the Cathedral. Its architecture is solid and low and unshakeable – such a contrast with the sinuous flow of the Nave, which succeeded it in style 300 years later. Here the Romanesque columns, on which rest the semi-circular arches, containing the groined vaulting, make us feel contained and safe.

It is a natural place to leave a lighted candle and write a prayer – here in its quiet, mystical, subdued light. If in the soaring architecture above us worries might be dissipated, here they can perhaps be concentrated, faced and defused.

*   *   *

Let us love the light, long to understand it and thirst after it; so that, led by it, we may come to it, and there live for ever.

[St Augustine of Hippo, Commentary on St John's Gospel 18:34]

*   *   *

At the centre of the Western Crypt is another altar, dedicated to the Blessed Virgin Mary when the first alteration and extension of Lanfranc's original building had been completed in 1130.

The sculptures of the capitals of the columns of the arcades are among the earliest of their kind and may depict beasts and symbols from pre-Christian religion. Here there is a symbol of fertility, and there the foliage of growth and natural life. But for the sculptors they may well have lost their symbolism, and become part of a decorative scheme.

The 14th-century screening of the Chapel of Our Lady Undercroft

Five different Masters have been identified in the various techniques and styles. It is a good place to reflect on the basics of religious life and thought, here among the foundations of a mighty Christian edifice.

This Crypt was once the favourite haunt of Edward Plantagenet – 'The Black Prince'. Edward was the youthful hero of England in the 14th century, and it was he who screened the Virgin's altar, with its lovely decorations, and refashioned as his chantry the transept now separated off as the Huguenot Church. Like him, countless others have been, and are, drawn back to this part of the Cathedral to find perspective and meaning for their lives. In its entirety the Crypt is a specially holy place. Unlike the Martyrdom, whose holiness comes from a traumatic event, the holiness of the Crypt emanates from beneath, welling up from the very origins of life and creation. Small wonder it evokes so much from within us.

*   *   *

Praise now to the keeper of the Kingdom of Heaven, the power of the Creator, the profound mind of the glorious Father, who fashioned the beginning of every wonder, the eternal Lord.

For the children of men he made first heaven as a roof, the holy Creator. Then the Lord of mankind, the everlasting Shepherd, ordained in the midst as a dwelling place, Almighty Lord, the earth for men.
Caedmon's Hymn (7th century)*

The Earliest English Poems (3rd Edition), trans. Michael Alexander, Penguin 1991.

The Eastern Crypt

Here we are taken on a few years architecturally. In many ways one feels a sense of release from the old restraints represented in the Western Crypt. Stout double-drummed columns interspersed with innovative pointed arches support a strong ribbed vault. Some eighty years have elapsed since the first eastern extension was begun. A catastrophic fire in 1174 had gutted the Quire above, and more space was needed in which to set a shrine for St Thomas. In a simple, rectangular undercroft on this site the body had lain since the day after the murder. Pilgrims were coming in increasing numbers to seek the help of the Saint. A protective structure was erected over Thomas's tomb and the new, much enlarged, eastern arm was built around it in a fresh style, rising to enfold the stately Trinity Chapel above. There the body was eventually taken on 7th July 1220, to be placed in the magnificent shrine prepared for it.

Meanwhile, the prayers of the faithful were rising in company with those of their Saint as his body rested here in the Eastern Crypt. Miracles attributed to his intervention and help were recorded by the monks in charge of the tomb, and then, in due course, portrayed in the glass of the Miracle Windows of the Chapel of the Shrine above.

There is a feeling of transitoriness about the Eastern Crypt. In many ways it is like finding an empty tomb. The process of enshrinement was one in which a body was raised from the grave to symbolic glory on its great catafalque. Acclaimed by the Church as numbered with the host of heaven, the remains of a saint became the relics of one whose salvation was assured and patent. Resurrection and immortality were demonstrated by raising up and proclaiming sacred.

Many of the unknowns and questionings and bewilderments with which graves confront us gain new and refreshing perspectives in the words of Jesus, which aptly come to mind here:

'I, if I be lifted up ... will draw all men unto me.'
[John 12:32, *AV*]

A sculpture from the Romanesque pulpitum screen, hidden for centuries in the infill of the walls of The Great Cloister

6

St Gabriel's Chapel

All of the side chapels of the Cathedral have their own charm and atmosphere. Their dedications make special connections with particular saints and here in the Crypt their character reflects strength and quiet security.

A distinguishing feature of St Gabriel's Chapel is that it is not dedicated to a human being, accredited by the Church as a saint, but to an angel – in fact one of the three named archangels of the Scriptures, of whom the others are Michael and Raphael. Angels and archangels in the Christian tradition are the heavenly beings who constitute the court of heaven. This court is in constant attendance upon God in worship and praise. Our own worship is united with this eternal offering and we are specially aware of it in glorious moments of the liturgy such as the Sanctus of the Eucharist: 'Holy, Holy, Holy Lord, God of power and might, heaven and earth are full of your glory'. As God's angels they have also been deemed to function as guardians of the faithful and as messengers.

Two of the occasions when St Gabriel acted as a messenger are represented in the paintings which cover the walls and dome of the apse in this chapel. To the left is the scene of the naming of St John the Baptist and to the right – sadly nearly obliterated – the announcement to the Blessed Virgin Mary of her conception of Jesus. In the centre, Christ is shown in majesty, surrounded by swirling angels, his hands dropped and spread in readiness to receive his worshippers. We feel quite strongly here the influence of Byzantine art. Contemplation of these paintings, flanked by the powerfully loving figures of Ezekiel's angelic vision on each side, draws us into the stillness of mystical prayer – venturing beyond the familiarities of human life into the divine mysteries of which angels are hints and glimpses.

*   *   *

Other medieval wall-paintings can be found in the Chapel of St Anselm above this one, where we will end this tour, and also in the north aisle of the Quire, where there is a large 15th-century painting of the Vision of St Eustace.

Decorative overpainting in this Chapel and elsewhere in the Crypt is the work of the Huguenot community, who were granted rights of usage in their exile in the 16th century.

The two block capitals of the columns are something of a foil to the mystique of the apse paintings. The superb 12th-century sculptures are very earthy, with their grotesque creatures intent on enjoying themselves. Contemporary manuscripts in the archives show the same scenes and it is a matter of speculation as to which copied which.

One of the faces of the central capital shows a donkey playing a lyre, which is a common image of the time of the sculptures. A fable of Phaedrus tells of a donkey finding a lyre in a meadow. In its frustration with its vain attempts to play it, the animal remarks: 'I do not know music, but if someone else had found this lyre, he would charm the ear with divine harmonies.'

Brought together in this Chapel, angelic paintings and beastly sculptures unite in a strange way the things of heaven and the things of earth. The mighty and transcendent God and his ordinary, often eccentric, creation are so different, yet complementary.

*   *   *

The icon in this Chapel was painted by Fr Luke of Chevetogne Abbey in Belgium. This is a monastery which enjoys close ties with Canterbury Cathedral. The icon represents the Annunciation to the Blessed Virgin Mary. The evil snake is shown nailed to the Tree of Knowledge, whose forbidden fruit Adam and Eve had taken, thereby, by their disobedience, separating human beings from untrammelled relationship with God. Mary's obedience balanced that sin and made possible the disclosure of God within his world in Jesus. The fountain of the water of life, shown below, is thus enabled to flow freely for those who likewise obey God. Christ in majesty presides over all. His left hand defers to his mother, towards whom his eyes are turned, and his right hand is falling in the act of blessing. He is flanked by the sun and the moon, which are ancient symbols of the creative complementations within life and creation.

*　　*　　*

The iron gate at the entrance to this Chapel contains some 12th-century wrought ironwork. One pauses to reflect that through this entrance, and over other thresholds into side chapels in the Cathedral, have passed countless priests over the centuries on their way to the altars within them. Such was the centrality of the service variously called the Mass, Eucharist, or Holy Communion, to the function of the priest in the medieval world that each day he was required to celebrate it. There was a need therefore, in a religious community of many priests, for many altars to meet the daily demand. In this way side chapels came into being as satellites of the High Altar which dominates the main part of the church.

Day by day, the different altars of the side chapels continue to be used for the Eucharist here in this Cathedral, each in its turn and with its own particular character. Daily, the small, representative congregation restates and renews the great Christian truth of the Word becoming flesh and dwelling among us. It is a truth of God, alive in his world and among his people – a truth which affirms the perfect harmony of heaven and earth, which is the ideal and purpose of life. These daily celebrations are microcosms of the great celebration, Sunday by Sunday, of the whole people of God, gathered at his table.

*　　*　　*

Word-made-flesh, by word he maketh
Bread his very flesh to be;
Man in wine Christ's blood partaketh:
And if senses fail to see,
Faith alone the true heart waketh
To behold the mystery.

St Thomas Aquinas 1227-74
Translated J M Neale 1818–66 and others

7

The Quire

The Quire of Canterbury is very large and, though begun by Archbishop Anselm, perhaps reflects the earlier ambitions of Archbishop Lanfranc. The ideal complement of 150 monks was only rarely attained in the six centuries of Benedictine life here. At the time of the dissolution of the monastery in 1540, fifty-three remained. Of these, twenty-eight were appointed to various offices of the New Foundation, which was to be governed by a Dean and twelve Prebendaries. The last Prior, Thomas Goldwell, was pensioned off, together with the other twenty-four monks. He was the only Prior of an existing monastic cathedral of England not to be made its new Dean.

Today the Dean and Chapter is composed of a dean and four residentiary canons, each having responsibility for particular aspects of the Cathedral's life.

Within the complexity of the great church, the Quire is the focus and symbol of liturgy and worship. It thereby represents the first obligation of God's people, which is the hallowing of God's name.

The High Altar dominates. This is the place where ordinary items of food – bread and wine – are taken and blessed, in obedience to Jesus' command. The form and ceremony which surrounds this essentially simple act is contrived to give full significance to the implications of the mystery involved. It is a mystery which results in the faithful partaking of the body and blood of Christ.

Another dominating furnishing is the brass lectern (1663), which bears the Holy Bible, the volume of the sacred scriptures of the Church. Open for all to see, it rests on an eagle, the king of birds whose high, soaring flight represents the soaring ascension of Christ and the soul rising in love to God. In these writings truths of God are revealed for human beings to learn, to understand and to live by.

The inward-facing stalls replaced 17th-century seating in 1879 and were designed by Sir George Gilbert Scott. The 17th-century return stalls remain, facing up the Quire towards the altar, and are the formal seats of the Dean and Chapter.

Two great thrones also make their presence felt. The high-canopied stone one (1848) at stall level is that in which the Archbishop is placed as Bishop of his diocese of Canterbury. The lone and ancient Throne of St Augustine (1220), high up behind the High Altar, is that in which he is placed as Primate of All England and Metropolitan, as well as to signify his presidential authority in the Anglican Communion.

In the presence of all these powerful symbols, representing historical origins and contemporary responsibilities, the strong pulse of the daily worship of God is maintained. The community is ever mindful that even more than being a great church, the Cathedral is also a place of spiritual resource, constantly being drawn on and in need of continuous replenishment. The members of the Foundation, visitors, pilgrims and those who pray towards this place day by day throughout the world, feed this great reservoir of spiritual strength on which so many depend.

There is a restless vitality about the architecture of the Quire, reaching through into the chevet of the open arcading of the Trinity Chapel beyond the Throne of St Augustine. Peculiarly known in Britain as 'transitional', it is of a style which sits between the Romanesque of the Crypt below and the perfected Perpendicular Gothic of the Nave. The simple ribbed vault above contrasts with the complex arcades supported by the drums of the columns below. The strong sculptures of the acanthus-leaved capitals, great and small, are almost tentative in their settings here, conveying a feeling of restraint.

In the construction of this great Quire early explorations were being made of the use in conjunction of the ribbed vault, the pointed arch and the unseen external flying buttress. These were the three devices which revolutionized European architecture in the 12th century and created the great Gothic cathedrals of western Christendom.

Apart from the lovely stone screens, added in 1304 by the great Prior Henry Eastry who ruled the monastery from 1285 to 1333, all here is as left by the builders in 1184. Their task had been one of massive refurbishment and extension after the fire of 1174.

Throughout Europe this was a time of new freedoms, in art and literature, in theology and philosophy, in politics and urban life, as well as in architecture. Old restraints were being shaken off and new forms discovered. Some have called it the '12th century Renaissance'. Change, development and innovation were in the air. It was an exciting era and the Quire picks up the vitality of it, and excites a sense of expectation.

*   *   *

Like as the hart desireth the water-brooks:
so longeth my soul after thee, O God.

My soul is athirst for God, yea, even for
the living God: when shall I come to appear
before the presence of God?

[Psalm 42: 1, 2, *BCP*]

8

The Corona

The termination of the great eastern arm of the Cathedral is architecturally extremely unusual, if not unique. From the outside it rather gives the impression of being an after-thought and it is clearly unfinished. The present somewhat clumsy castellation was formed in the 18th century from an unfinished extra storey of about 1530, and the original intentions of the 12th-century builders remain unclear. It feels as though it should be a tower, which to some extent it is, in a truncated form. The existing western towers and the central Bell Harry tower, together with the two smaller tow-ers attached to the eastern transept, plus two more which were intended to flank the Presbytery and which were part-ly built and then reduced shortly after – all of these, togeth-er with this eastern one, would have made a many-towered Cathedral indeed.

However, the Corona was built, in the first instance, for a practical purpose, and that was to contain the reliquary holding the piece of Thomas's skull which was cut off by a sword blow when he was murdered. It is often referred to as 'Becket's Crown'.

In medieval times this chapel was the penultimate 'station' kept by the pilgrims, before they finally arrived at the great shrine itself. The reliquary was almost certainly in the form of a silver-gilt bust with the piece of bone placed in the head. It was the last moment for the pilgrim to recall the sacrifice of the Saint's life before turning to his glory, proclaimed by the bejewelled shrine nearby.

The interior of the Chapel has a fine and satisfyingly simple symmetry in its circular form. Maintaining the theme of sacrifice, it is now dedicated to the Saints and Martyrs of Our Own Time. Commemorative books on each side carry photographs and remembrances of a representative few, who show that martyrdom continues to be a fact of life. Day by day people of faith die for the sake of Jesus and the truths of God that he proclaimed and which they have espoused.

The frontal of the altar was made in 1982 by Joyce Conway-Evans and is embroidered with words from T. S. Eliot's *Murder in the Cathedral*:

> The Blood of Thy
> Martyrs & Saints
> shall enrich the earth,
> shall create
> the Holy places

This is a place in which to recall the cost of standing for what is right, and to thank God for people who do so with that extreme courage which is born of deep convictions. Such witnesses participate in the ongoing suffering of God, as it was shown by the crucifixion of Jesus, his beloved Son. It is a mutual suffering, of God and his people, which will continue so long as evil has any place in the life of the world.

This is another place in the Cathedral where candles are lit and left as deposits of prayer. Their flaming supplications remind us of lights of witness in a world which so often feels dark and overpowering.

One of the names in the commemorative books is that of Dietrich Bonhoeffer, who was executed, after considerable suffering, in a Nazi concentration camp. While there he often used a prayer of Paul Gerhardt (*c.* 1607–76):

> Every Christian in his place
>   should be brave and free,
>   with the world face to face.
> Though death strikes, his spirit should
>   persevere, without fear
>   calm and good.
> For death cannot destroy
>   but from grief brings relief
>   and opens gates to joy.
> Closed the door of bitter pain,
> bright the way where we may all heaven gain.

From Dietrich Bonhoeffer,
Letters and Papers from Prison.

*   *   *

The tomb on the left is that of Cardinal Reginald Pole, archbishop (1556–8) during the time after the Reformation when, briefly, the country returned to acknowledging Papal authority in the Church. He was a holy and gentle man, who had little stomach for the political machinations into which he was drawn.

To the right is the monument of Frederick Temple, appointed at the age of seventy-five, and archbishop for six years (1896–1902). He was greatly devoted to social concerns and fostered the causes of temperance and education. He did much to extend the work of the Church in foreign missions, and the text of his last sermon in the Cathedral was:

'Woe is unto me if I preach not the Gospel.'

[I Corinthians 9:16, *AV*]

Later his son, William, was to follow him as archbishop (1942–5).

Ancient Stained Glass

The 13th-century central window of the Corona Chapel has come to be called the Redemption Window. It is one of many typological, or Bible, windows put into the Cathedral at this time. They were so called because events of the Gospels are shown surrounded by foreshadowing 'types' from the Old Testament. So, in this window, the saving acts of Jesus – his crucifixion, burial, resurrection, ascension, and the descent of the Holy Spirit at Pentecost – occupy the central panels. Around each of these are four other panels of Old Testament 'types'. For example, one of the types for Jesus' burial is the fish consuming Jonah, and one of the types for Jesus' resurrection is the fish belching Jonah out on to the shore [Jonah 1:17 and 2:10]. Detailing these events and their associations gave great scope for teaching, and other 'Bible Windows' of the same kind are found in the north aisle of the Quire.

Although Canterbury has a wealth of stained glass of various periods, it is the medieval stained glass that is one of its greatest treasures. A 12th-century genealogical series encircled the whole of the clerestory from the central tower eastwards. There were eighty-four figures, from Adam onwards, which constituted the human ancestry of Jesus' family. These are now spread around the Cathedral in other positions and replaced with 18th-century replicas.

Another series (13th-century) was that of the Saints of Canterbury. These were at triforium level in the aisles of the Quire. St Dunstan and St Alphege remain on the north side.

The most famous series of all were the 13th-century 'Miracle Windows' which surrounded the Trinity Chapel, container of the Shrine, depicting miracles attributed to the intervention of Thomas.

From the 13th-century Redemption Window

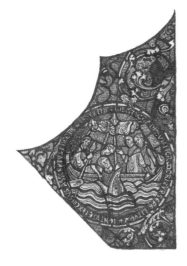

Jonah is thrown overboard and swallowed by the fish

Jonah is belched out on to the shore

9

The Trinity Chapel
Site of St Thomas's Shrine

This Chapel is really a massive casket, created to contain what had come to be the most precious possession of the Cathedral, the body of Thomas Becket. The jewels of the casket are the richly coloured 13th-century windows surrounding it. The frame is one of stone, shaped, sculpted and set, with all the potential of later, perfected Gothic architecture within its construction, struggling to emerge. Viewed from outside the Chapel is a graceful shape, with its chevet and pitched roofs falling away from peak to clerestory to aisle – a massive chasse, well-proportioned and ornamented.

Within the Chapel lay that which it was created to contain – the ornate shrine of a hero of the faith. It was one of the major attractions of medieval European devotion and tourism, and one of those places where you could be certain that time and eternity met. Pilgrims came in penitence to Canterbury, so as to be joined hand in hand with the 'holy, blissful martyr' so favoured by God. The undertaking of a penitential pilgrimage was a declared commitment to amending one's life according to the faith of the Saint, and carried its own spiritual credit.

The great shrine remained here from 1220 until 1538, when it was destroyed on the orders of King Henry VIII, and its treasures plundered. Estimates suggest that it stood some ten feet high overall, on a plinth eight feet long by four feet wide. We have several descriptions from those who visited it, and from their accounts we know that, over the years, its furnishings and embellishments were changed from time to time.

A gold-plated casket was set on a pink marble base, which in its turn was placed on a plinth of three grey, stone steps. The central area of the now bare Chapel retains the stones of those steps in its paving. The golden casket was embellished with precious stones, and many carried their own stories, each explained to important visitors by the custodian monks. Most famous of all was the Regale of France, a massive ruby given by Louis VII in 1179.

At the western end of the shrine was an altar, and the whole was enclosed by protective iron railings. Before the altar was the magnificent pavement of Opus Alexandrium, probably made by the Cosmati workshop in the 13th century, and possibly the gift of Henry III. It is made up of sections of porphyry and marble, cut from columns and stones taken from even more ancient buildings, and remains as one of the Cathedral's great treasures. The path of the pilgrims' feet, filing past the shrine, is evident in the indentation worn in the stones of the floor on each side.

Other relics were kept in chests on a beam over the altar. There were large square candles high up and the sanctuary light, which always burned, was provided by a roll of waxed candle which the town of Dover was obliged to maintain. Way above, in the vault, were pennants and battle standards which were memorabilia from the Crusades, and recall that at one time Thomas was entitled 'Thomas of Acre'. The remaining crescent is thought by some to be a last vestige of those battle honours, though it is perhaps more likely that it was the crescent moon at the feet of the painting of the Blessed Virgin Mary which, it is said, occupied that particular web of the vault.

The gold-plated coffin was covered by a painted wooden case which, in its turn, was overhung with a woven canopy and hangings. The cover was raised at certain times of the day to enable adoration by the pilgrims. It is interesting that

The 12th-century Trinity Chapel, created to contain the shrine of St Thomas of Canterbury

the popularity of pilgrimage to Canterbury was by no means consistent. We can pick up, from surviving accounts of takings at the various Cathedral pilgrim stations, an ebb and flow in the numbers over the years. Certainly in the 15th century a general decline had set in. Attitudes were then changing and the amazing sight of the treasure-laden space, which we get from the impressions of visitors of the time, became more of a public spectacle than an icon of devotional focus. The Venetian ambassador, visiting in 1496, wrote, '… the magnificence of the tomb of St Thomas the Martyr, Archbishop of Canterbury, is that which surpasses all belief'.

Now a solitary candle burns on an open, bare floor inscribed as shown opposite. The magnificence has long gone, but the mysterious wonder remains. Pilgrims have always been drawn to Canterbury and always will. The holy places associated with Thomas, set within the great holy space, are, in their turn, spots where people will always want to pause and pray. At the Martyrdom we recognise the supreme Lordship of Jesus Christ among people and their affairs. At the place of the first tomb we pray for faith in God and the assurance of resurrection. At the Corona we give thanks for the courage of the saints and renew our commitment.

When we come to the place of the Shrine itself we stand on the threshold and look from the thrall of the seen, known and material of time into the freedom of the unseen, unknown and mysterious of eternity. It is just as it was for the disciples when Jesus was taken from them at his ascension into heaven. It is just as it is when we approach God in prayer and gaze into mystery. The Shrine confronts us with the challenge of belief and the demand of faith. Looking up, and then down the length of the simple ribbed vault of the Quire, through to the delicate vanes of the

THE

SHRINE

OF

THOMAS

BECKET,

ARCHBISHOP

AND

MARTYR

STOOD

HERE

FROM

1220

UNTIL

1538

colonnade of the Nave, the human spirit is taken on its continuing journey from the hope and the aspiration of what is, into the satisfaction and the glory of what is to come.

*   *   *

Almighty God,
   give us the courage of Thomas the Martyr and the
   faith of the saints. In your mercy lead us forward
   with confidence through life and death, following
   our Lord and Saviour, Jesus Christ.

10

St Anselm's Chapel

Our time in the Cathedral ends in a chapel in which the remains of one of the greatest figures of the Christian Church are laid to rest. It was the vitality of his faith, complemented by intellectual rigour, expressed in care for his fellows, and coupled with warmth as a person and a deep, personal relationship with God, that made St Anselm such a complete Christian.

In the large, modern (1959) window which dominates this chapel, the Saint is shown as the central figure, flanked by personages important to his life. Close to him, on the left, is Archbishop Lanfranc. Lanfranc had been Anselm's tutor when he was a junior monk. Little did either of them realize that they would both be archbishops of the great See of Canterbury, and that the pupil would succeed his master. Close to him, on the right, is Baldwin, who was a fellow monk, and Anselm's friend and physician.

On the outer flanks are two kings. William II (Rufus), on the left, was the monarch who urged Anselm to become Archbishop in the face of the Saint's reluctance and resistance. He would have much preferred to remain living the life of a monk in community. Out to the right is Henry I, William's successor, and the other king in whose reign Anselm served. With both kings the Archbishop had deep differences, and at various times was driven into exile by each over political issues.

Anselm's Chapel is a good place in which to pause and reflect for a while, before leaving this great Cathedral. Already we have felt an atmosphere of power. The artistic vision and skilled craftsmanship which made this building are the result of it. Behind everything is the power of the presence of God himself. Through his whole creation, but above all through his people and their works and ways, God's presence is evident in his world. Where we become aware of him, in things and in people, we do well to pause and take notice. If we allow ourselves to relax and become still, we will become even more aware of him, and he will speak to us with hope and guidance and reassurance.

The Lord has many voices. In a great Cathedral he speaks through the events of its history as well as through its on-going life and worship. People of the past and people of the present come together to make a timeless community. Those who were the great and good of the centuries past, rub shoulders with those who are the ordinary and day-to-day of the present, in the common cause of commitment to Jesus Christ. Such commitment is at the same time their love of God and their love of their fellow human beings. In the vitality of that faith, Christianity is both nurtured and pro-created.

Some people pass through the building quite quickly and go on their way having scored another visit to a place to be 'done'. Even so, few of them will entirely forget. Others have some particular focus of interest – the glass perhaps, or monuments, or the music, or the monastic history. Few of them will forget. Others are gripped and held and changed by a sense of a great presence, resonating within them. Such people will never forget. Indeed, some will never be the same again and will remember for ever.

Look down to the simple inscription in the floor –

ANSELM

It is picked out in the green marble of Aosta, the place of the Saint's birth and youth. There his spiritual life began at the age of five with a vision in which he was received into the court of heaven and the presence of God. The truth of this experience was always with him and its mystical message was never lost.

Before worrying and struggling to understand God, we must first take the step of allowing ourselves to believe in him. He is greater than any human attempt might envisage or understand. Almighty, loving, and embracing of all, his arms are spread wide to receive and enfold those who turn to him in thanksgiving and praise.

*   *   *

Lord, I am not trying to make my way to your height,
for my understanding is in no way equal to that,
but I do desire to understand a little of your truth
      which my heart already believes and loves.

I do not seek to understand so that I may believe,
but I believe so that I may understand;
      and what is more,
I believe that unless I do believe I shall not
      understand.

[*The Prayers and Meditations of St Anselm*,
trans. Sister Benedicta Ward, SLG]

*   *   *

Conclusion

Leave this lovely and holy place with renewed vision and hope. Remember the sacrifice of the Saints and, like them, endeavour to serve God in love and care for others.

> May the love of God enfold you
>   and may Thomas and the Saints of
>   Canterbury pray with you,
>
> May your holy guardian angel
>   watch over you,
>
> May you be blessed with peace
>   and fulfilled in Christ, so
>   that finally you may be gathered
>   into the worship of heaven.

An angel from the Chapel of Our Lady Martyrdom